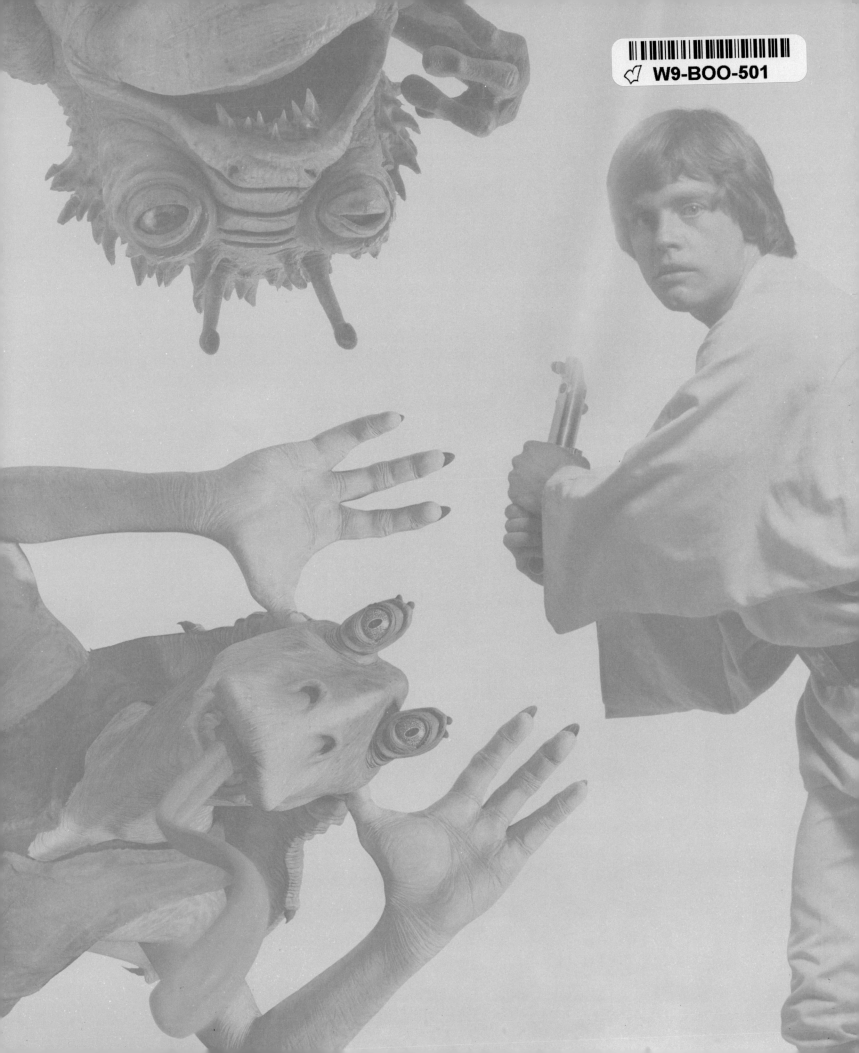

# THE
# AMAZING
# BOOK OF
# STAR WARS

Written by Elizabeth Dowsett

Look out for fun questions throughout the book.

# Introduction

Welcome to a galaxy far far away. Here you will find all sorts of strange people, alien creatures, droids and vehicles. Some are good, some are bad, and for some, it can be hard to tell if they are good or bad. But they are all amazing.

# CONTENTS

# FRIENDLY DROIDS

**Which droid rolls like a ball?**

Lift the flap to find out!

**Sensor for smelling**

**Electrical wires**

**Oiled knee joint**

## C-3PO

C-3PO is a shiny gold protocol droid. Protocol droids help people understand each other. C-3PO can speak more than six million languages.

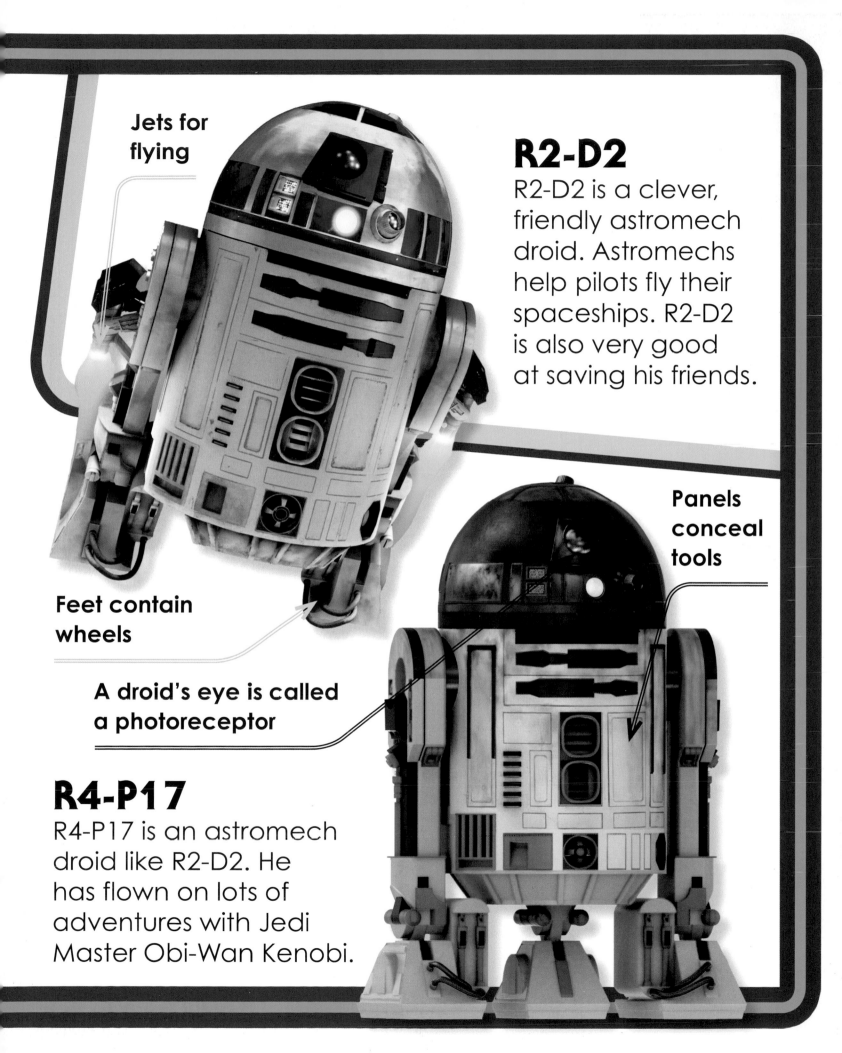

Jets for
flying

# R2-D2

R2-D2 is a clever,
friendly astromech
droid. Astromechs
help pilots fly their
spaceships. R2-D2
is also very good
at saving his friends.

Panels
conceal
tools

Feet contain
wheels

**A droid's eye is called
a photoreceptor**

# R4-P17

R4-P17 is an astromech
droid like R2-D2. He
has flown on lots of
adventures with Jedi
Master Obi-Wan Kenobi.

# Yoda

Wise Yoda is more than 900 years old. Don't be fooled by his small size. He is the most powerful Jedi and the best at lightsaber battles!

**Large green ears**

**Two-handed grip on lightsaber**

# Mace Windu

All across the galaxy, Mace Windu is respected for his wisdom. When this calm, powerful Jedi talks, people listen.

**Simple Jedi robes**

# JEDI MASTERS

Headtails

Natural
Togruta
colour

## Shaak Ti
Shaak Ti is skilled at
fighting. Her hollow
headtails sense the
space around her
so she can duck out
of danger quickly.

Kit's lightsaber
is waterproof

Head
tentacle

## Kit Fisto
Kit Fisto can breathe in air
and water. He senses feelings.
This makes him a good friend,
but also a fearsome warrior.

# Young Anakin

As a child, Anakin Skywalker surprises everyone with his skill with the Force. He loves to fly machines in really fast races called podraces.

**Flying goggles**

**Flying helmet**

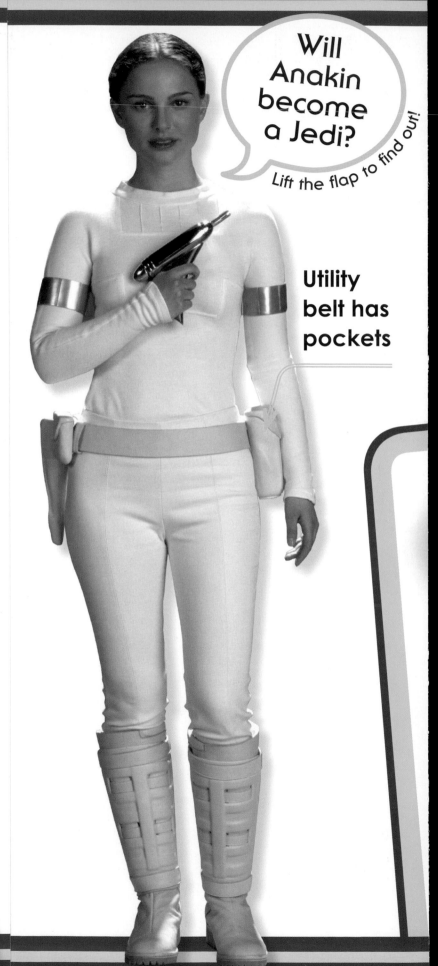

Will Anakin become a Jedi?

Lift the flap to find out!

**Utility belt has pockets**

# BRAVE HEROES

Blue blade is powered by a blue crystal

Jedi tunic

Tool belt

## Obi-Wan Kenobi
Wise Obi-Wan Kenobi is Anakin's Jedi Master. He's a skilled warrior, but he prefers to win by using words rather than by fighting.

**Coloured visor**

## Clone Pilot
Clone soldiers who show particular talent are given extra training to become pilots. They fly gunships and spaceships.

**Tube carries air**

**Machine helps pilots breathe**

# Clone Trooper

Clone troopers fight with the Jedi to protect the galaxy. They are grown in a factory and are all identical to each other.

**Binoculars**

**DC-15 blaster rifle**

**Basic white armour**

**Would you like to be a clone?**

**Belt with pockets**

**Armour is hinged so leg can bend**

# ARC Trooper

A few clones are trained for special missions. They are called ARC troopers and they have red marks on their armour.

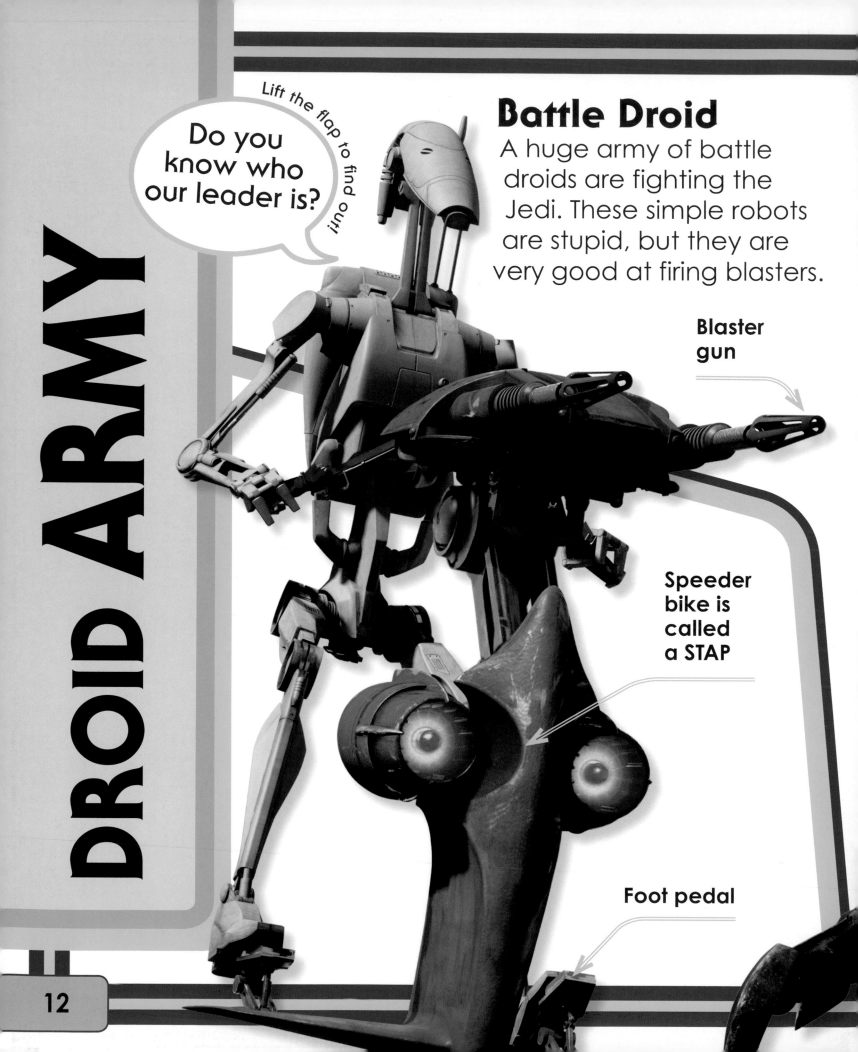

# DROID ARMY

Do you know who our leader is?

Lift the flap to find out!

## Battle Droid

A huge army of battle droids are fighting the Jedi. These simple robots are stupid, but they are very good at firing blasters.

Blaster gun

Speeder bike is called a STAP

Foot pedal

# Super Battle Droid

Super battle droids are the muscle of the droid army. They are bigger, stronger and tougher than regular battle droids, but they are just as stupid.

**Blaster bolts shoot from wrist**

**Extra thick armour**

**Shield for protection**

**Blaster fire**

# Droideka

Beware these rolling droids of war! Droidekas wheel onto the battlefield, then uncurl to reveal their deadly blasters.

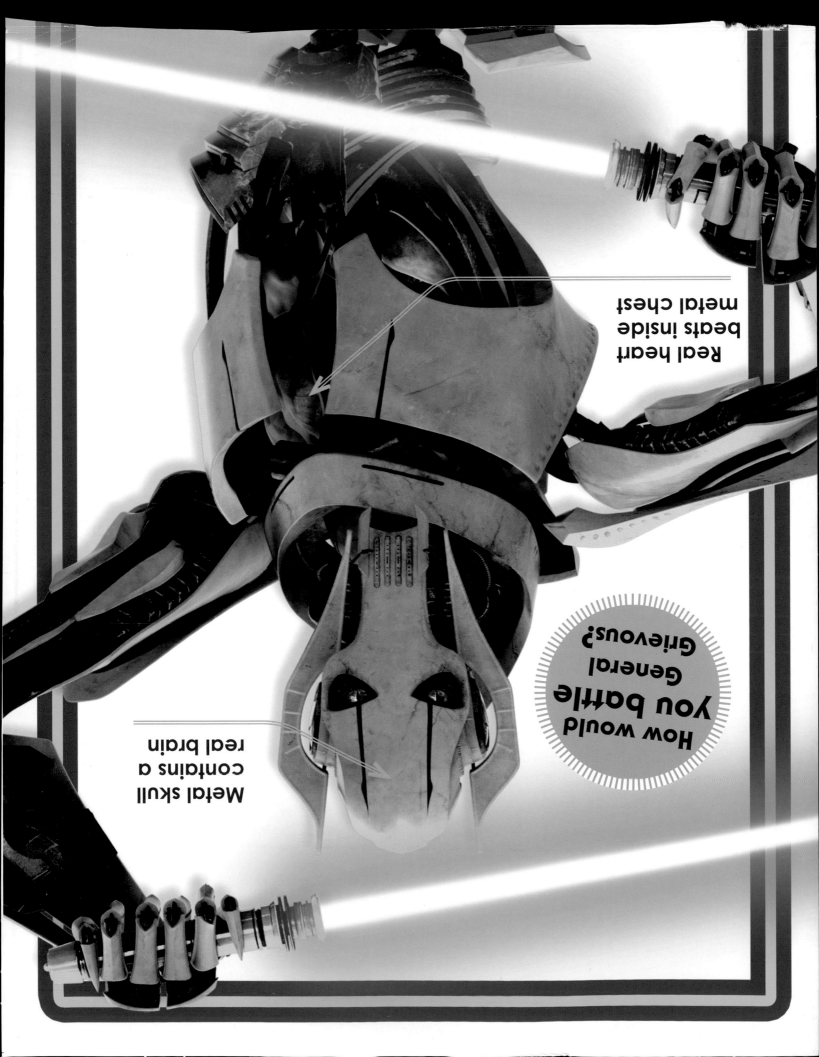

Real heart
beats inside
metal chest

Metal skull
contains a
real brain

How would
you battle
General
Grievous?

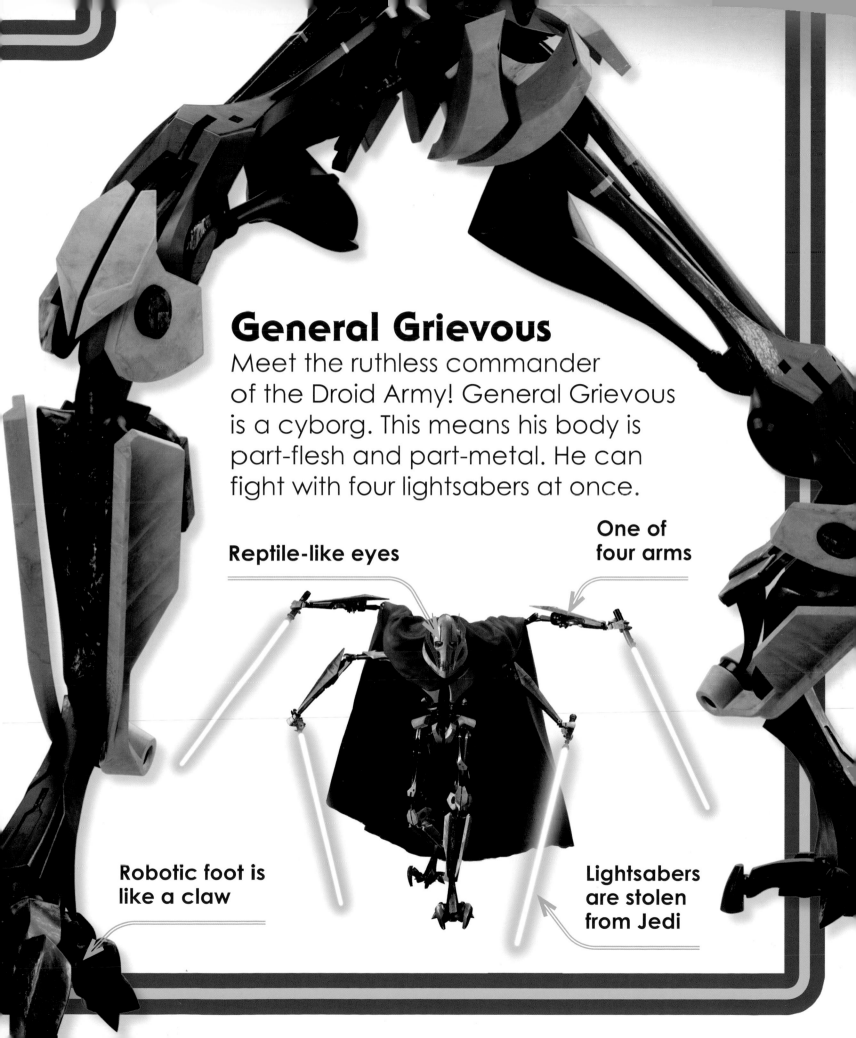

# General Grievous

Meet the ruthless commander of the Droid Army! General Grievous is a cyborg. This means his body is part-flesh and part-metal. He can fight with four lightsabers at once.

**Reptile-like eyes**

**One of four arms**

**Robotic foot is like a claw**

**Lightsabers are stolen from Jedi**

**Shell encases droid in flight**

## Buzz Droid

Buzz Droids are little metal menaces. They cling to your spacecraft, then attack it with their tools until it crashes.

**Spikes attach to ship**

## Dwarf Spider Droid

These four-legged machines scuttle into battle with the Droid Army, armed with a deadly laser cannon.

**Eyes glow red**

**Hinged legs move like a spider's**

14

# Tri-fighter

Tri-fighters fire lasers and buzz droids. They are small enough to dodge big ships, but are powerful enough to destroy them.

**Body carries buzz droids**

**Laser cannon**

# Crab Droid

Crab droids are six-legged weapons used for ground battles. They have armour like a crab shell and they shoot lasers.

**Tough armour**

**Feet move well through mud**

## Max Reebo

Feel the rhythm with this blue Ortolan. He is Max, the leader of the Max Reebo band, and he loves to play the red ball jet organ.

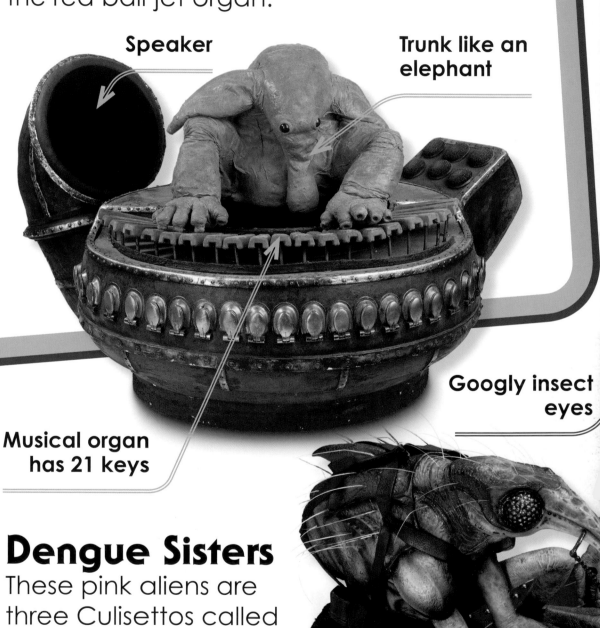

**Speaker**

**Trunk like an elephant**

**Googly insect eyes**

**Musical organ has 21 keys**

## Dengue Sisters

These pink aliens are three Culisettos called the Dengue Sisters. They love to play the game Deia's Dream.

Large eyes have no eyelashes

Band's uniform

# Figrin D'an

Figrin D'an plays in a music band with six other Bith. Bith are bald, bug-headed creatures who are intelligent, peaceful and musical.

Loose frocks for travelling

Instrument is called a kloo horn

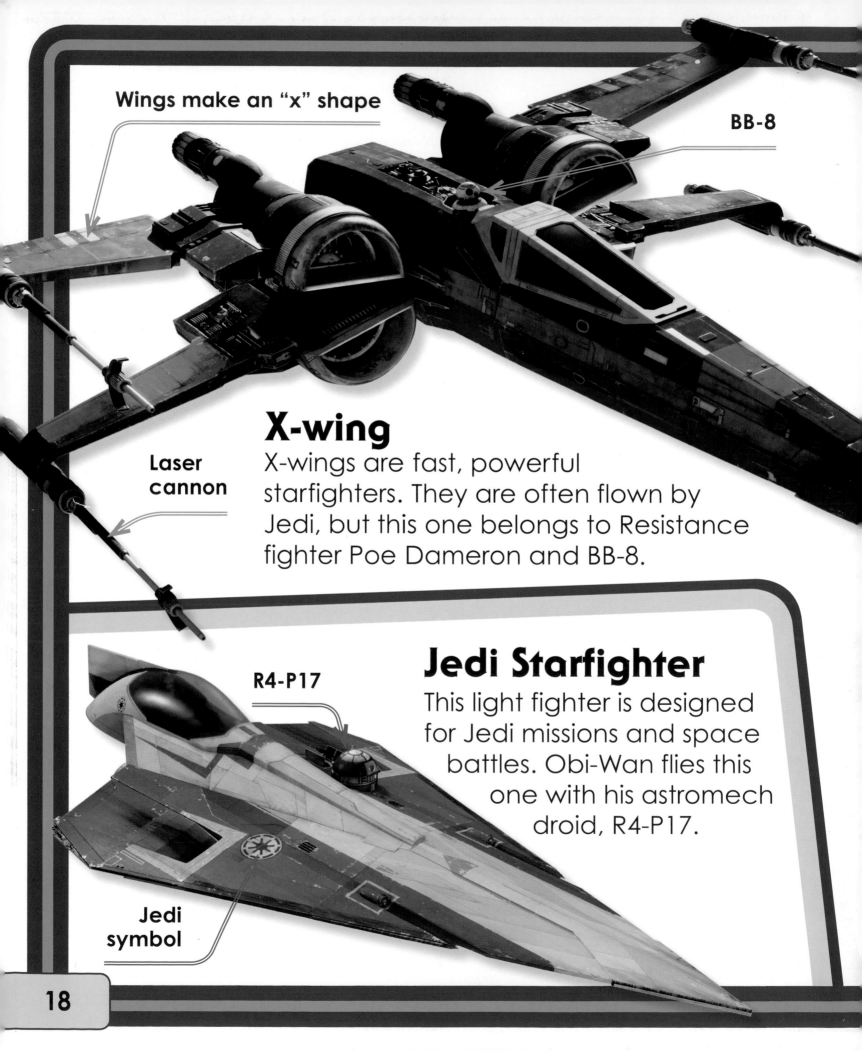

Wings make an "x" shape

BB-8

Laser
cannon

# X-wing

X-wings are fast, powerful
starfighters. They are often flown by
Jedi, but this one belongs to Resistance
fighter Poe Dameron and BB-8.

R4-P17

# Jedi Starfighter

This light fighter is designed
for Jedi missions and space
battles. Obi-Wan flies this
one with his astromech
droid, R4-P17.

Jedi
symbol

# SPEEDY SHIPS

### Jedi Interceptor

Jedi Interceptors are small, speedy spacecraft. They fly best when piloted by Jedi using the Force, like Anakin and Obi-Wan.

**Wings fold**

**Ship is the shape of a capital "Y"**

**Ion cannons**

### Y-wing

Y-wings are powerful fighters and bombers. Rebel pilots fly them in many space battles against the Empire.

**Laser cannon**

Glowing eyes

## Gamorrean Guard

These green-skinned brutes make good guards. They aren't very smart, but they are loyal and like to fight.

Eyes don't see well

Sharp axe

*Lift the flap to find out!*

Are the Sith real?

Ion blaster

## Jawa

Don't leave anything lying around when jawas are about! These short, cloaked creatures will steal it and sell it on to make money.

# FEARSOME FOES

**Delicate wings**

**Sonic blaster**

## Geonosian Drone

These alien insects live on the dusty planet Geonosis. The drones are tough warriors who think only about fighting. They attack in large swarms.

**Who do you think is the scariest?**

## Zam Wesell

If you want to attack someone, you can pay Zam to do it for you. She can also change her body to look like any other creature.

**KYD-21 blaster**

**Key can open any lock**

# Happabore

Happabores look like a cross between a pig and a crocodile. They are very strong and are used for carrying heavy loads.

**Closed eye**

# Varactyl

Lizard-like varactyls can run fast and climb rocky walls. Jedi Master Obi-Wan rides one called Boga to chase General Grievous.

**Saddle**

**Powerful legs for running**

**Crest of feathers**

## Worrt

Squat, spikey Worrts live on desert planets. They hide in the sand waiting for insects to grab with their long tongues.

**Eyelid keeps sand out of eye**

**Spikey body**

**Teeth contain poison**

23

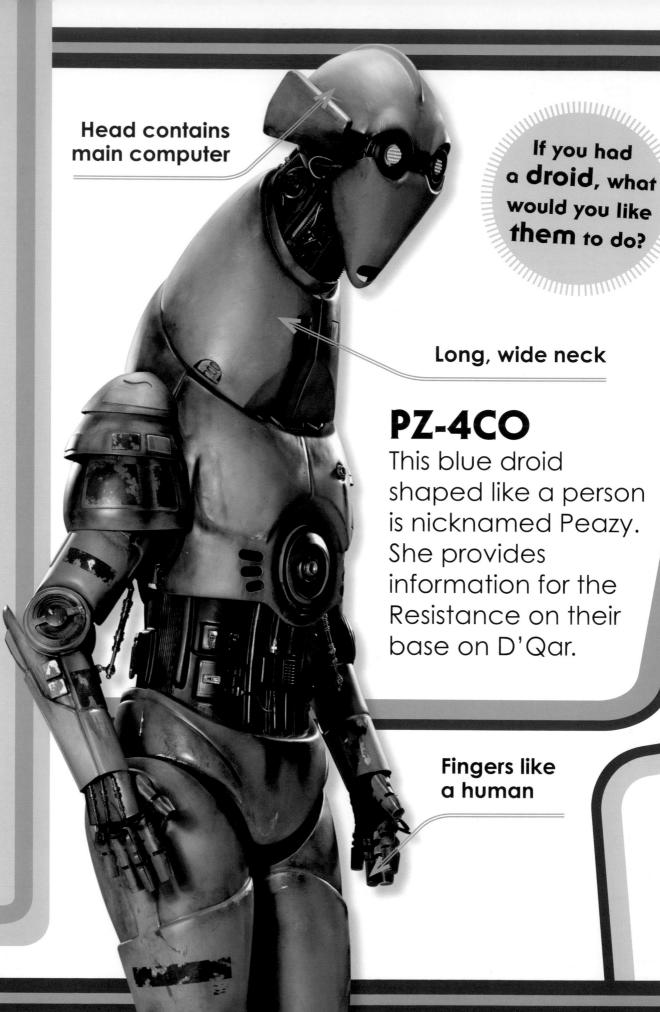

# WORKER DROIDS

Head contains
main computer

If you had
a **droid**, what
would you like
**them** to do?

Long, wide neck

## PZ-4CO
This blue droid
shaped like a person
is nicknamed Peazy.
She provides
information for the
Resistance on their
base on D'Qar.

Fingers like
a human

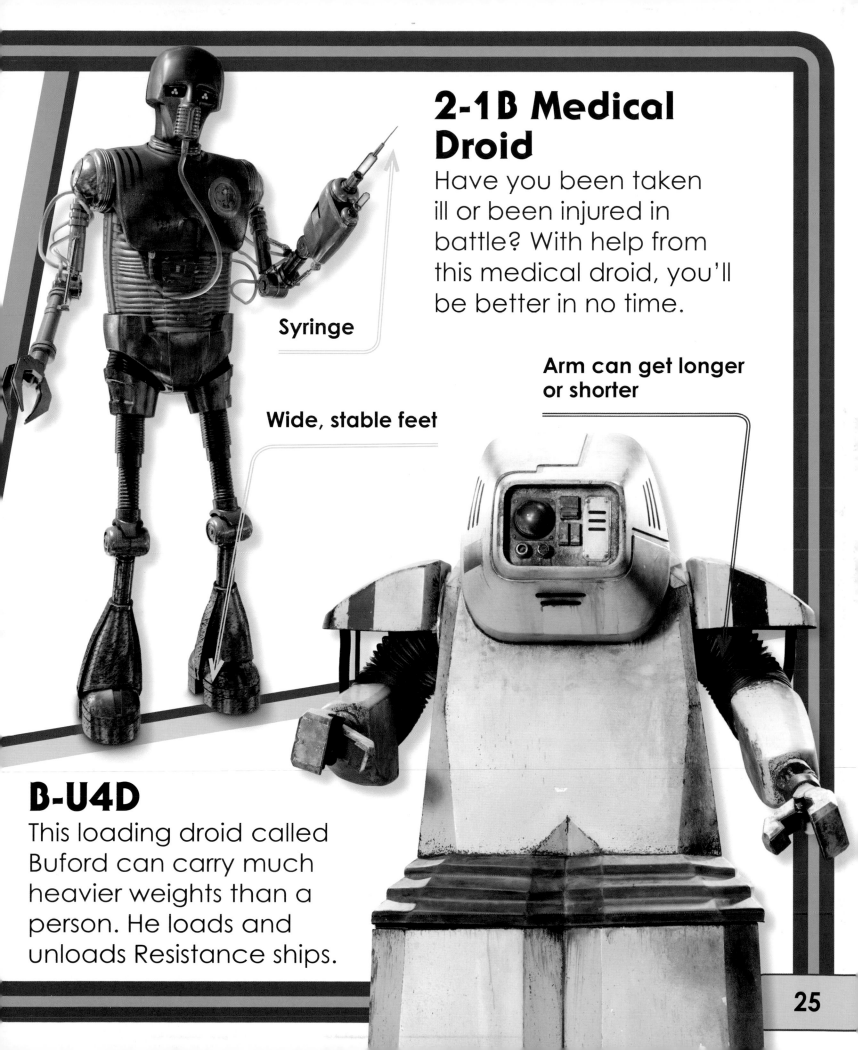

## 2-1B Medical Droid

Have you been taken ill or been injured in battle? With help from this medical droid, you'll be better in no time.

**Syringe**

**Arm can get longer or shorter**

**Wide, stable feet**

## B-U4D

This loading droid called Buford can carry much heavier weights than a person. He loads and unloads Resistance ships.

# EVIL EMPIRE

Lift the flap to find out!

Do you know who my Apprentice is?

## Emperor Palpatine

Beware this man! Palpatine is actually an evil Sith Lord called Darth Sidious. He has seized control of the galaxy and made himself Emperor.

**Skin damaged by the dark side of the Force**

**Large hood for hiding Palapatine's face**

# Young Boba

Young Boba is learning how to be a bounty hunter from his dad, Jango. His lessons are fighting, using weapons and tracking enemies.

What will I be when I grow up?

Lift the flap to find out!

**Hands are ready for fighting**

# Boba Fett

Boba Fett grows up to be a ruthless bounty hunter. Like his father, Jango, he can fly in the air using the jet pack on his back.

**Guns on wrists**

Flight suit

Bullet-proof vest

Rangefinder folds down over visor

Would you like to be a **bounty hunter?**

Strong, double-layered flight suit

## Bossk

Bossk is a vile lizard who enjoys hunting people. He doesn't care what's good or bad. He just works for whoever pays him the most.

EE-3 blaster rifle

# Watto

Watto buys and sells junk like scrap metal and droid parts. He always cheats people if he can. Watto is Anakin's owner, until Anakin wins his freedom.

**Wings flap very fast**

**Data pad**

**Webbed feet**

# Jabba the Hutt

Jabba is a huge, toad-like Hutt. His favourite things are power and money. Many criminals work for him, and he lives in an enormous palace.

**Body crawls like a snail**

**Helmet contains breathing equipment**

# Stormtrooper

Millions of stormtroopers serve the Emperor. They are tough soldiers who fight without questioning orders.

**Narrow black visor**

**E-11 blaster**

**Staff for fighting is called a force pike**

# Imperial Royal Guard

The Emperor's best soldiers can become his personal bodyguards. They are also known as the Red Guard because of their long red robes.

Sith lightsaber
glows red

# Darth Vader

Darth Vader is powerful in the dark side of the Force. He's Emperor Palpatine's Sith Apprentice, and he's very dangerous.

Would you like to work for Darth Vader?

Mask hides Vader's scarred face

Suit keeps Vader's injured body alive

# IMPERIAL ARMY

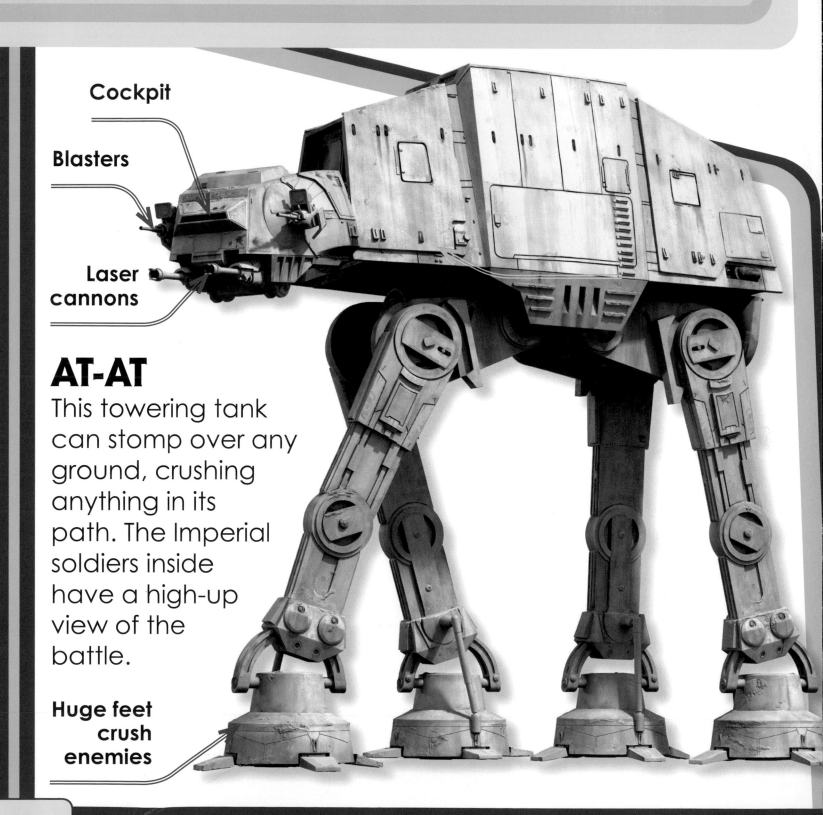

Cockpit

Blasters

Laser cannons

## AT-AT

This towering tank can stomp over any ground, crushing anything in its path. The Imperial soldiers inside have a high-up view of the battle.

Huge feet crush enemies

# Speeder Bike

Speeder bikes zoom easily over uneven ground. They're a fast way for scout troopers to get around muddy planets, but they need to look out for trees!

Sensor helps bike avoid obstacles

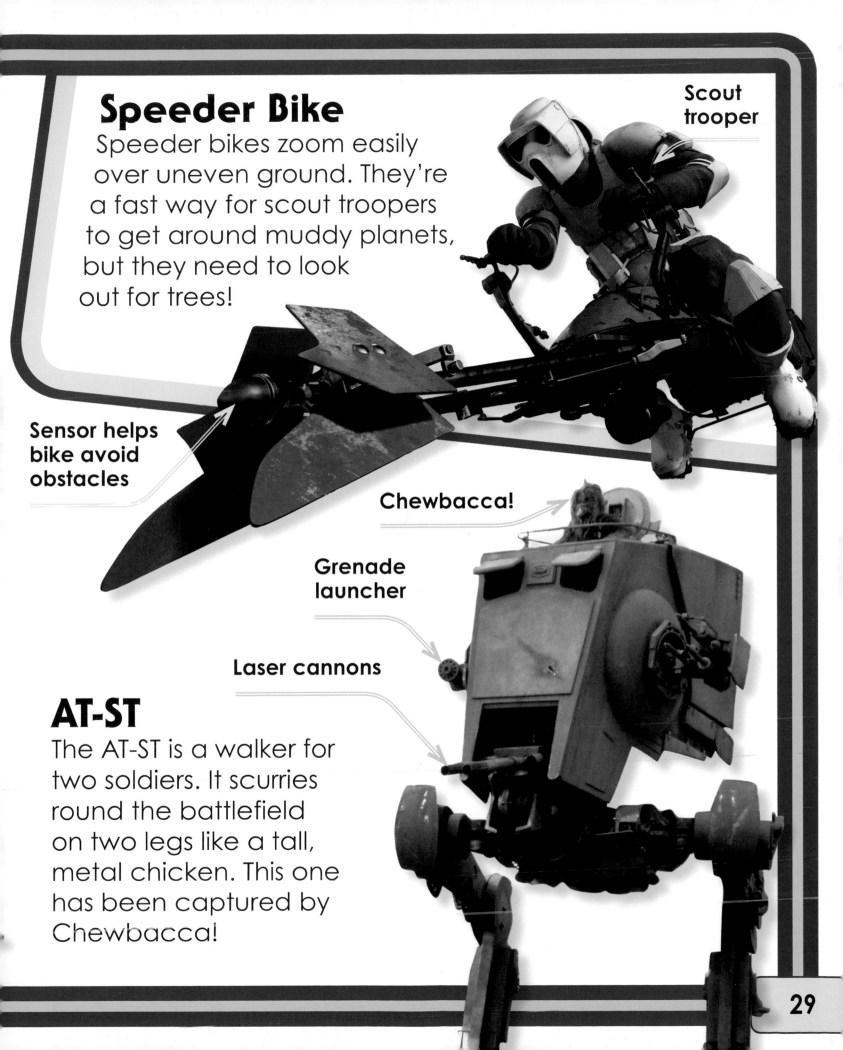

Chewbacca!

Grenade launcher

Laser cannons

# AT-ST

The AT-ST is a walker for two soldiers. It scurries round the battlefield on two legs like a tall, metal chicken. This one has been captured by Chewbacca!

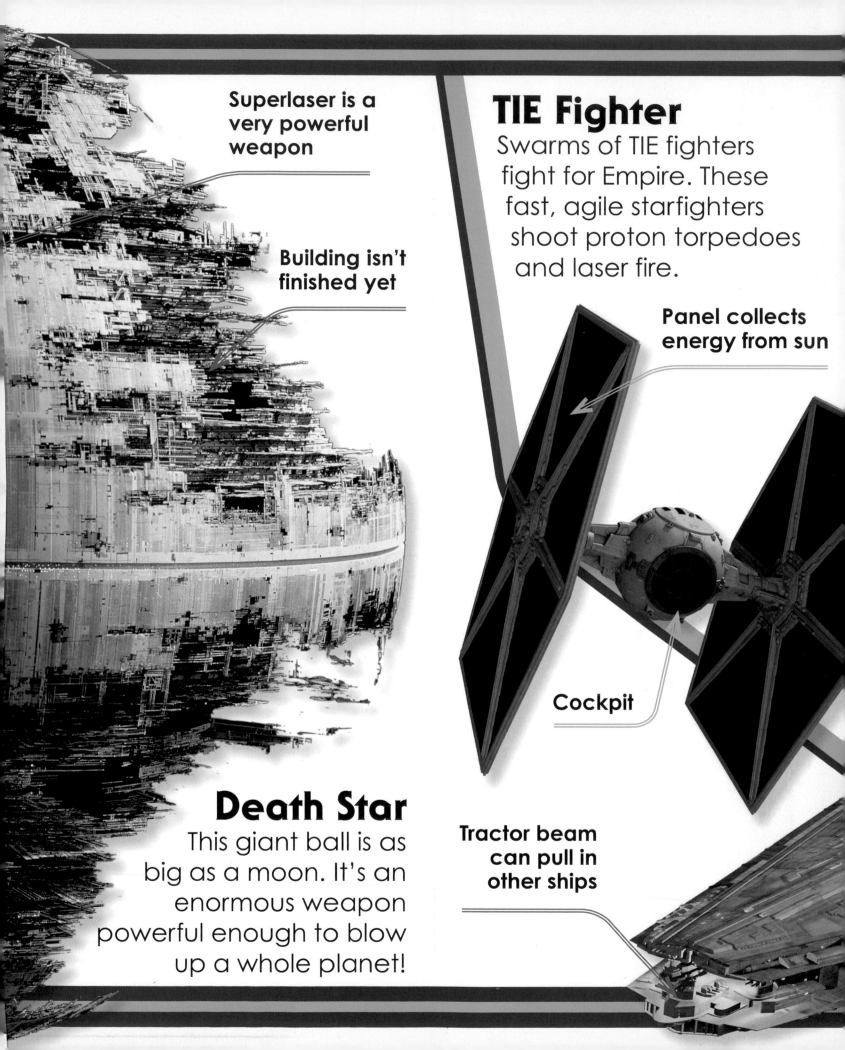

**Superlaser is a very powerful weapon**

**Building isn't finished yet**

# TIE Fighter
Swarms of TIE fighters fight for Empire. These fast, agile starfighters shoot proton torpedoes and laser fire.

**Panel collects energy from sun**

**Cockpit**

# Death Star
This giant ball is as big as a moon. It's an enormous weapon powerful enough to blow up a whole planet!

**Tractor beam can pull in other ships**

Symbol of the Empire

Tubes carry air to helmet

Life-support system

# TIE Pilot

TIE fighter pilots are specially trained to fly TIE fighters for the Empire. They wear special black flight suits that keep them alive in space.

# WAR MACHINES

## Star Destroyer

Behold the largest ship in the Empire's fleet! The huge dagger-shaped Star Destroyer is a symbol of the Emperor's great power.

What's the Empire's new secret project?

Lift the flap to find out!

**Command bridge**

**Hangars contain many TIE Fighters**

Nose is very sensitive like a dog's nose

# Chewbacca

Hairy Chewbacca is a Wookiee from the planet Kashyyyk. Strong and loyal, he is Han Solo's friend and co-pilot.

Blaster stolen from the Empire

Bandolier contains ammunition

# Han Solo

Han is always getting into trouble trying to make money. Happily, he's good at getting out of trouble, too, and he helps the rebels.

Gun holster

# BRAVE REBELS

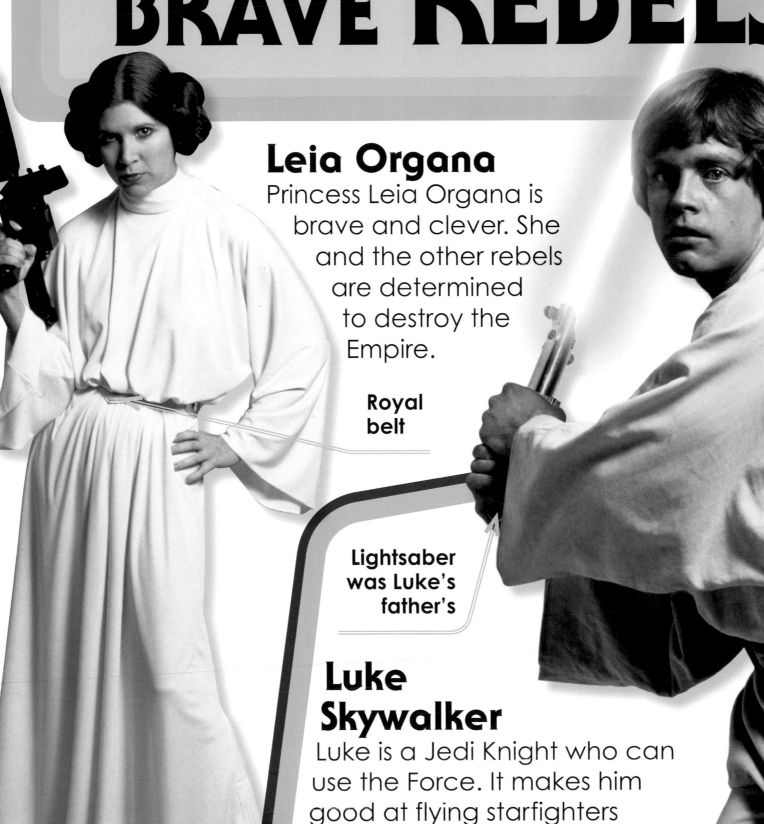

## Leia Organa

Princess Leia Organa is brave and clever. She and the other rebels are determined to destroy the Empire.

**Royal belt**

**Lightsaber was Luke's father's**

## Luke Skywalker

Luke is a Jedi Knight who can use the Force. It makes him good at flying starfighters and fighting with his lightsaber.

# AWESOME SHIPS

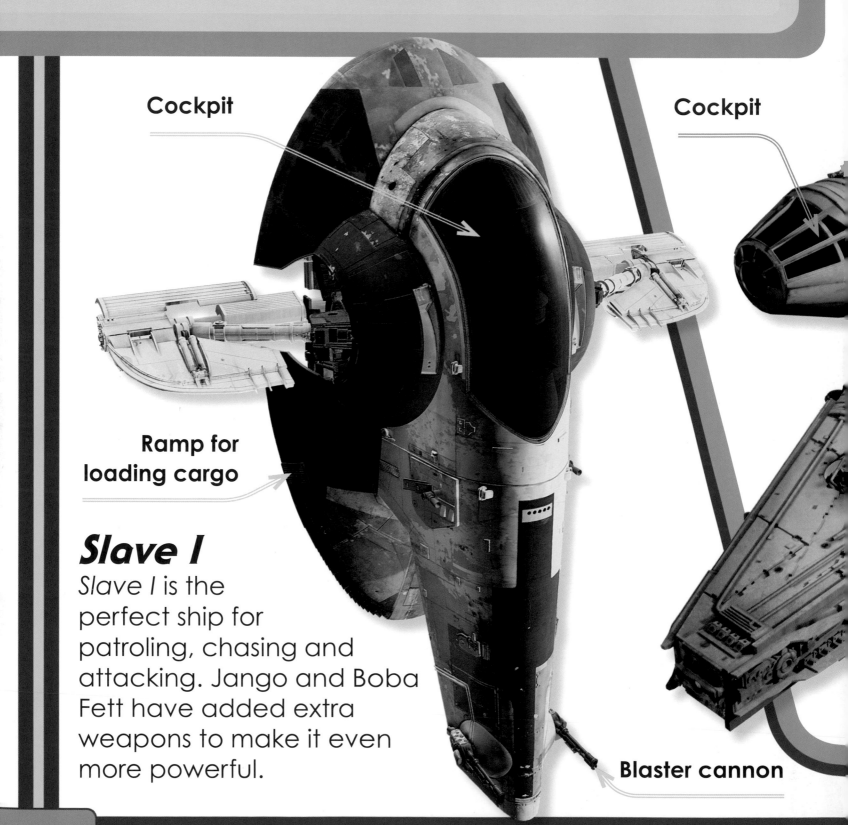

Cockpit

Cockpit

Ramp for loading cargo

## Slave I

*Slave I* is the perfect ship for patroling, chasing and attacking. Jango and Boba Fett have added extra weapons to make it even more powerful.

Blaster cannon

# Millennium Falcon

The *Millennium Falcon* looks like a flying heap of junk, but it's the fastest ship in the galaxy. It has helped Han Solo escape trouble many times.

Which **ship** would you like **to fly?**

Battle damage

## Jango Fett

Jango Fett is one of the most feared bounty hunters in the galaxy. All clone troopers are copies of him.

**WESTAR-34 blaster**

**Sniper rife**

**Gauntlet shoots darts**

**Head contains a computer**

**Short-range pistols**

**Extra-long fingers**

## Aurra Sing

Cruel Aurra Sing is a sniper and can use a lightsaber. She helps train Boba Fett after his dad is killed in battle.

36

# VILE VILLAINS

## Sebulba

Sebulba loves to podrace, but he's not to be trusted. He does everything he can to hurt Anakin in the podrace, but he still can't beat him!

Magnifying glass

Metal apron

Would **you trust** any of these characters?

## Unkar Plutt

Unkar Plutt gives people like Rey food in exchange for scrap metal. He's mean and gives as little food as possible.

**Coins from winning races**

# ALIEN ALLIES

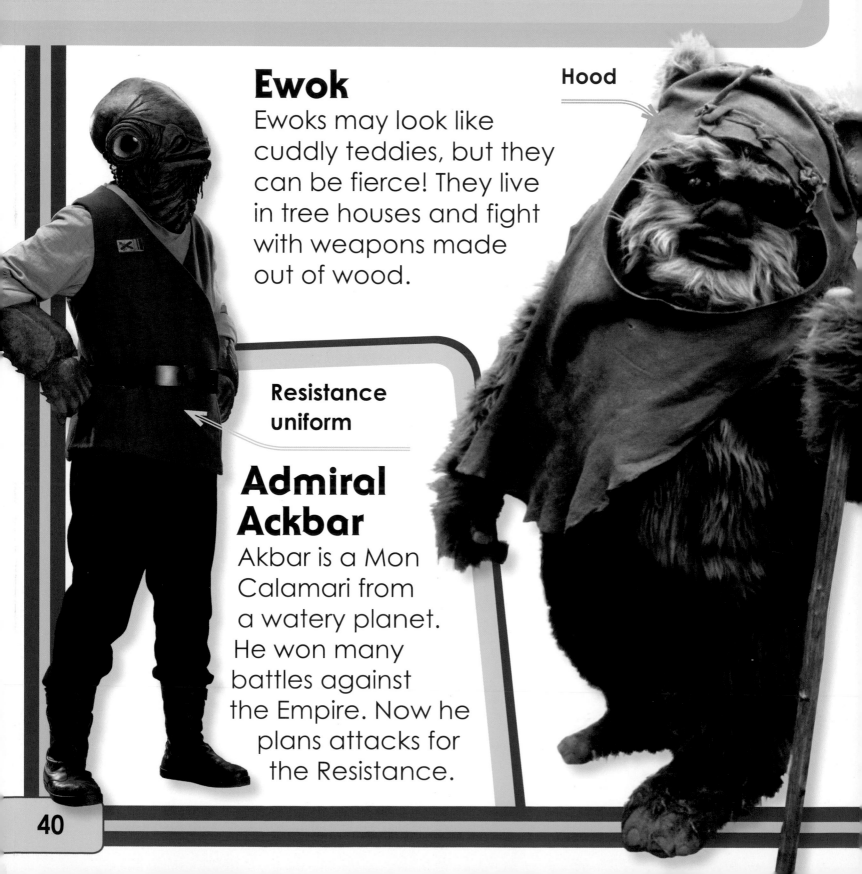

## Ewok

Ewoks may look like cuddly teddies, but they can be fierce! They live in tree houses and fight with weapons made out of wood.

**Hood**

**Resistance uniform**

## Admiral Ackbar

Akbar is a Mon Calamari from a watery planet. He won many battles against the Empire. Now he plans attacks for the Resistance.

Goggles help
Maz to see

Which
Gungan
helps the
Jedi?

Lift the flap to find out!

Spear for
hunting

Many jangly
bracelets

# Maz
# Kanata

Maz is a wise, old
pirate chief who
has had a long life
of adventure. She has
a connection with the
Force and is a friend
to the Resistance.

Wooly
socks
Maz
knitted
herself

# Kylo Ren

Kylo Ren is Leia and Han's son. He was training to be a Jedi, but was tempted by the dark side. Now he works for the scary First Order.

**Rare lightsaber with three blades**

# DARK POWERS

## Stormtrooper

These shiny white soldiers fight for the First Order. They have more high-tech armour than the stormtroopers who used to fight for the Empire.

**Weapon is called a megablaster**

**Blaster pistol in leg holster**

**Silver armour is only worn by Phasma**

## Captain Phasma

Captain Phasma leads the First Order's stormtroopers. She wants a strong, ruthless army, so she keeps a close eye on all her soldiers.

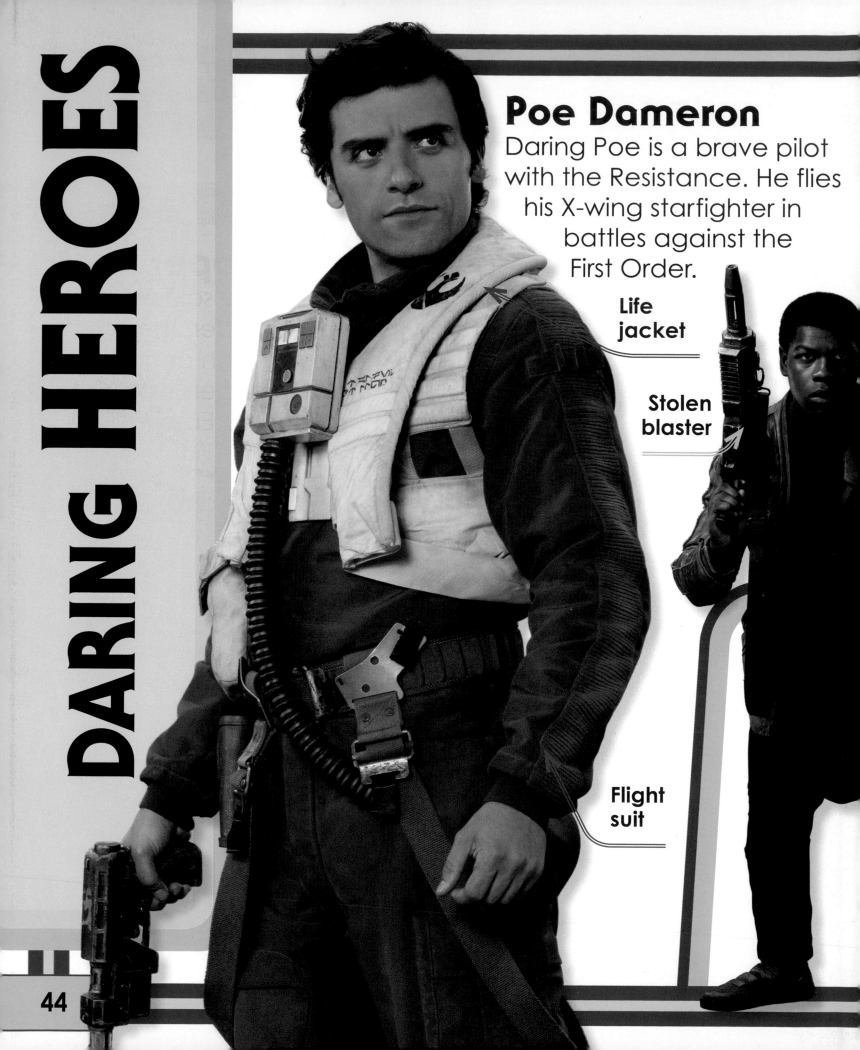

# DARING HEROES

## Poe Dameron

Daring Poe is a brave pilot with the Resistance. He flies his X-wing starfighter in battles against the First Order.

Life jacket

Stolen blaster

Flight suit

## Rey

Rey is a pilot, mechanic and skilled fighter. She is strong in the Force and is learning how to use it in order to fight the First Order.

**Clothes for the desert**

**Staff for fighting**

**Finn's fighter jacket**

**Explosive ball**

Would **you join the** Resistance?

## Finn

Being a First Order stormtrooper was all Finn knew, until one day he realised he was on the wrong side. He bravely escaped and joined the Resistance.

1 Who is the most powerful Jedi?

2 Who is Anakin's Jedi Master?

3 What colour are the markings on ARC trooper armour?

4 How many arms does General Grievous have?

5 What is this?

6 What colour is Max Reebo?

7 Which droid flies in Poe's X-wing?

8 Who has been secretly training in the dark arts of the Sith?

9 What is the name of the varactyl ridden by Obi-Wan Kenobi?

10 Who is this?

11 What colour robes do the Emperor's bodyguards wear?

12 What type of bird does an AT-ST look like?

# QUIZ

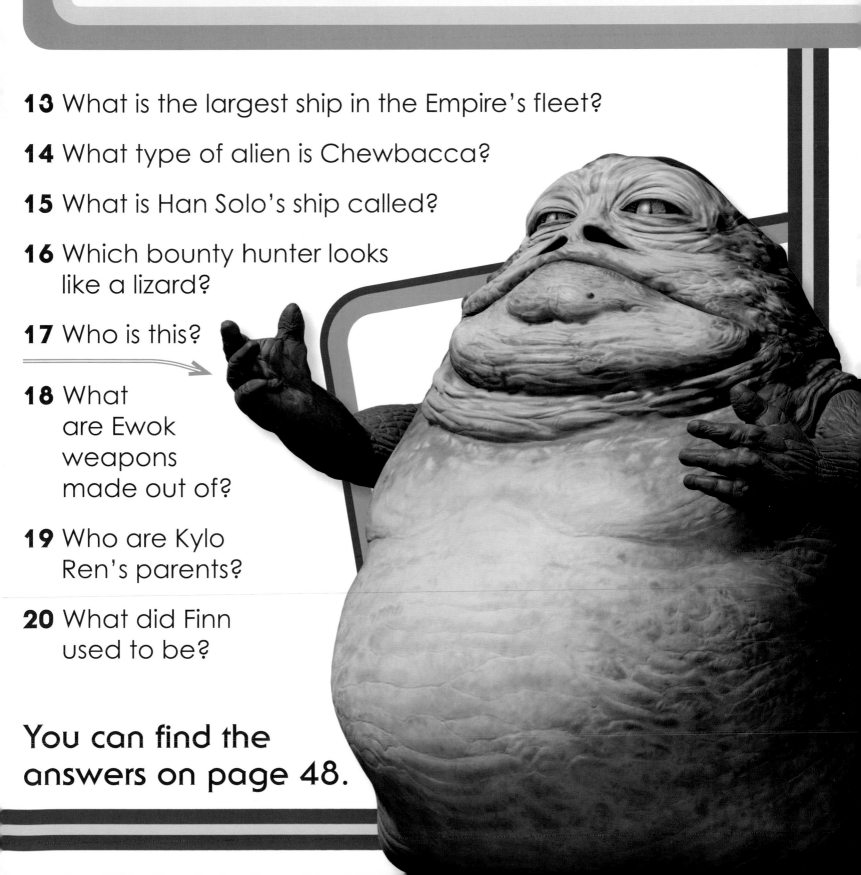

**13** What is the largest ship in the Empire's fleet?

**14** What type of alien is Chewbacca?

**15** What is Han Solo's ship called?

**16** Which bounty hunter looks like a lizard?

**17** Who is this?

**18** What are Ewok weapons made out of?

**19** Who are Kylo Ren's parents?

**20** What did Finn used to be?

You can find the answers on page 48.

**Senior Editor** Elizabeth Dowsett
**Senior Art Editors** Mabel Chan, Anna Formanek
**Designer** Anna Pond
**Senior Pre-production Producer** Rebecca Fallowfield
**Senior Producer** Alex Bell
**Managing Editor** Sadie Smith
**Managing Art Editor** Ron Stobbart
**Publisher** Julie Ferris
**Art Director** Lisa Lanzarini
**Publishing Director** Simon Beecroft

**Written by Elizabeth Dowsett**

## Answers to the quiz on pages 46 and 47

1 Yoda
2 Obi-Wan Kenobi
3 Red
4 Four
5 Buzz droid
6 Blue
7 BB-8
8 Darth Maul
9 Boga
10 Peazy/PZ-4CO
11 Red
12 A chicken
13 Star Destroyer
14 A Wookiee
15 The *Millennium Falcon*
16 Bossk
17 Jabba the Hutt
18 Wood
19 Leia Organa and Han Solo
20 A stormtrooper

First published in Great Britain in 2016 by
Dorling Kindersley Limited
80 Strand, London, WC2R 0RL
A Penguin Random House Company

10 9 8 7 6 5 4 3 2 1
001–295424–Oct/16

Page design copyright © 2016 Dorling Kindersley Limited

© & TM 2016 LUCASFILM LTD.

A CIP catalogue record for this book
is available from the British Library

ISBN 978-0-2412-6321-1

DK would like to thank Chelsea Alon at Disney
and Frank Parisi at Lucasfilm.

The author would like to thank Emily Dowsett, Reuben Akehurst,
Edward Allan, Finn Dowsett, Jake Dowsett, Harry Duggin,
Cormac Heinrich and Audrey Peyton-Nicoll.

Printed and bound in China

A WORLD OF IDEAS:
SEE ALL THERE IS TO KNOW

www.dk.com
www.starwars.com